D1456727

IMAGE SHARING

GLOBAL CITIZENS: SOCIAL MEDIA

Published in the United States of America by Cherry Lake Publishing
Ann Arbor, Michigan
www.cherrylakepublishing.com

Content Adviser: Marcus Collins, MBA, Chief Consumer Connections Officer, Marketing Professor
Reading Adviser: Marla Conn MS, Ed., Literacy specialist, Read-Ability, Inc.

Photo Credits: © Rawpixel.com/Shutterstock.com, Cover, 1; © SundayMorningPhoto/Shutterstock.com, 5;
© KC Slagle/Shutterstock.com, 6; © Sharaf Maksumov/Shutterstock.com, 8; © Lipik Stock Media/Shutterstock.com, 11;
© Mi.Ti./Shutterstock.com, 13; © tataev_foto/Shutterstock.com, 14; © tongcom photographer/Shutterstock.com, 17;
© LadyPhotos/Shutterstock.com, 18; © Dado Photos/Shutterstock.com, 20; © Dragon Images/Shutterstock.com, 23;
© Artem Varnitsin/Shutterstock.com, 25; © Chat Karen Studio/Shutterstock.com, 26; © LightField Studios/
Shutterstock.com, 28

Library of Congress Cataloging-in-Publication Data

Names: Orr, Tamra, author.
Title: Image sharing / Tamra B. Orr.
Description: Ann Arbor : Cherry Lake Publishing, [2019] | Series: Global citizens : social media |
    Audience: Grade 4 to 6. | Includes bibliographical references and index.
Identifiers: LCCN 2018035590 | ISBN 9781534143081 (hardcover) | ISBN 9781534139640 (pbk.) |
    ISBN 9781534140844 (pdf) | ISBN 9781534142046 (hosted ebook)
Subjects: LCSH: Photography--Digital techniques—Juvenile literature. |
    Digital images—Social aspects—Juvenile literature. | Social media—Juvenile literature.
Classification: LCC TR267 .O77 2019 | DDC 771/.4—dc23
LC record available at https://lccn.loc.gov/2018035590

Cherry Lake Publishing would like to acknowledge the work of the Partnership for 21st Century Learning.
Please visit www.p21.org for more information.

Printed in the United States of America
Corporate Graphics

ABOUT THE AUTHOR

Tamra Orr is the author of more than 500 nonfiction books for readers of all ages. A graduate of Ball State University, she now lives in the Pacific Northwest with her family. When she isn't writing books, she is either camping, reading, or on the computer researching the latest topic.

TABLE OF CONTENTS

CHAPTER 1
History: Strike a Pose... 4

CHAPTER 2
Geography: The Age of Selfies 10

CHAPTER 3
Civics: Photography Ethics 16

CHAPTER 4
Economics: Internet Advertising 22

THINK ABOUT IT... 30
FOR MORE INFORMATION...31
GLOSSARY 32
INDEX 32

History:
Strike a Pose

Smile! Say "cheese"! You're about to have your picture taken. You might be the photographer, perfecting that **selfie** pose, or snapping a photo of the food you ordered for lunch. In today's world, taking and sharing photographs is as much a part of the day as eating food, doing homework, or going to school.

In the past, taking a picture was a slow process. You had to have a camera with film in it. The film had to be purchased at a store. When you eventually took the picture, it was a gamble. Did you have poor lighting? Were your arms steady when you

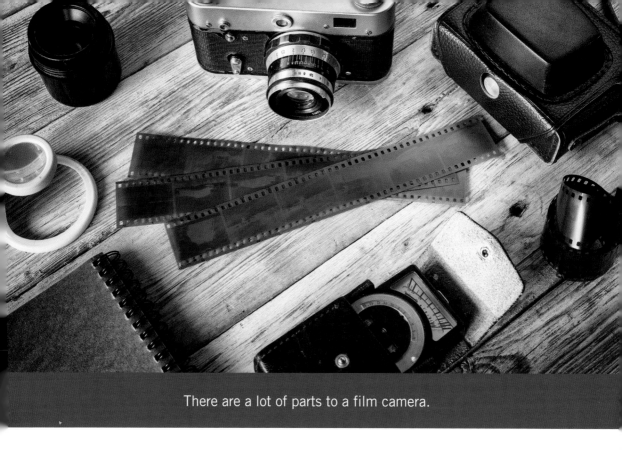

There are a lot of parts to a film camera.

took the shot? Was your finger in the way? You wouldn't know until you shot 24 or 36 pictures on the roll of film, **developed** it, and got the pictures back. It could take weeks to find out (if you didn't develop the film yourself). Then, if friends wanted copies of the picture, you'd have to request more prints to be made, which could also take a few weeks.

Instant cameras, popularized by Polaroid, produced images quickly, but you couldn't share them unless the photographs were photocopied or recreated by taking another photo!

Today, taking a photo doesn't require a camera (just a phone!), and you can instantly see the image you shot. Because of the internet and social media, you can share it, not just with friends and family, but also with the entire world.

The number of pictures being taken today is staggering. Every 24 hours, almost 2 billion photos are uploaded to the internet and shared on social media around the world. That is 83.3 million every hour—about 1.4 million per minute!

A History of Pictures

By the mid-1980s, people were able to send emails. But these were only text-based. Images could not be attached to them. When it first became possible to send images, they took so long to upload and attach to the email that it was rarely worth the effort. By the late 1990s, things had vastly improved. The very first image-sharing site, Shutterfly, was launched. In 2000, taking pictures became easier with the first built-in camera cell phone. Cell phones later turned into smartphones. Smartphones were even better at taking high-quality photos. Within a few years, phones were able to take photos almost as good as high-end digital cameras. With this came a surge of social image-sharing platforms. In 2009, Facebook added a new dimension to sharing photos: being able to tag people in them!

Imgur, an image sharing site, was originally created to share images on Reddit.

More image-sharing sites launched—and ended. Many early platforms were designed with a theme in mind, some more specific than others. DailyBooth (no longer active), for example, was designed for people taking a photo every single day. Foodspotting (no longer active) was for showing off and recommending recipes and gourmet dishes. Pinterest was designed for people to discover and share information and ideas through images, **GIFs**, and videos. By 2011, iPhones and Android phones had special apps for taking better pictures. You could use stickers or fun **filters**, make a collage, or creatively crop images. Some social image-sharing platforms even allow you to add hashtags, GIFs, and so much more.

Developing Questions

Have you ever spent time checking out world averages? How often does a person change their socks? How frequently does someone purchase something online? Averages can be interesting to study. Do you do something more or less often than the average? For example, the average number of times a day a person under age 21 checks their phone is 46. How often do you check yours? More or less? Keep track of a few of your habits for a few days. Log how many times you stop to take and share an image. Once shared, do you check your post often to see how many likes you gathered? What does the frequency tell you about your social media life?

Geography: The Age of Selfies

Guess what picture experts believe most **millennials** will take more than 25,000 times during their life? Their dog? What about their best friend? Pizza? Nope! (Although, pizza is the most popular food featured on Instagram.)

The answer? Themselves! These pictures, known as selfies, are similar to the self-portraits many artists, from Leonardo da Vinci to Andy Warhol, have painted and sculpted. (But selfies are faster, easier, and far less expensive.) Selfies are also one of the most shared images found on the internet.

Studies report that 87 percent of people between the ages of 18 and 34 have taken a selfie and uploaded it to a social networking

Language experts believe the word "selfie" originated from Australia, as it is common for Australians to add "-ie" to their words, and an Australian man unintentionally made the word go viral.

site. Although the average age of selfie-takers is 23.6 years old, that number will drop as more preteens and teens begin snapping their self-portraits.

While it is clear young people are crazy about taking their own photos, it may come as a surprise that the United States is not the top selfie-taking country. *Time* magazine did a study of more than 400,000 digital selfies to see where the majority of them came from. It may surprise you.

Selfies around the World

Picture a world map. Can you guess which city across the globe is known for having the most selfie-takers? The answer is Makati City in the Philippines. A city of 500,000 people, it has earned the nickname of the "Selfie Capital of the World." Which cities follow? The second-most popular city of selfies is New York's Manhattan, followed by Florida's Miami. Other countries on the top 10 selfie list include Malaysia (Petaling Jaya and George Town), Israel (Tel Aviv), England (Manchester), and Italy (Milan). Which cities came

Most Popular on Instagram

Without a doubt, celebrities get the most followers on image-sharing sites, like Instagram. Singer Selena Gomez has 138 million, followed by soccer player Cristiano Ronaldo with 132 million followers. The current record for the single post getting the most "likes" (or hearts) goes to Kylie Jenner. When she posted the first photo of her baby on Instagram, she got almost 14 million "hearts" in less than 24 hours! The most popular selfie (so far!) on Twitter was taken by Ellen DeGeneres at the 2014 Oscars. The photo featured a dozen stars, including DeGeneres, Bradley Cooper, Meryl Streep, Julia Roberts, and Brad Pitt.

According to historians, the first selfies were self-portraits—the first painted around 1523–1524 by Italian artist Girolamo Francesco Maria Mazzola (also known as Parmigianino).

PARMIGIANINO

In Moscow, Russia, women take about 82 percent of selfies in the area!

in last on *Time*'s list of 459 locations? Bakersfield, California, and Staten Island, New York, were at the bottom, along with Nice, France. (In France, selfies are often referred to as "braggies"!)

Selfies are rarely (or never) taken or shared in a few countries, including China, Turkey, Iran, North Korea, and Vietnam. These countries are known for banning social media platforms, including those dedicated to sharing images.

Speaking of Banning . . .

Anyone who takes selfies knows about selfie sticks. These long sticks allow people to take self-portraits from more of a distance. However, in a growing number of places, these tools are being banned for safety reasons. Shockingly, dozens of people have died when reaching for that perfect shot. They have fallen off cliffs, been killed by wild animals, or suffered something equally as horrifying while angling for that picture-perfect shot. Because of this, all Disney parks ban selfie sticks. Not surprisingly, using a selfie stick during the **running of the bulls** in Pamplona, Spain, is not allowed. More and more outdoor concerts and festivals are also asking their fans to leave their sticks at home.

Gathering and Evaluating Sources

How can you tell when something shifts from being a temporary trend or fad to something that has lasting impact on the culture? One way is if the word describing the trend make it into the official Oxford English Dictionary. In 2013, "selfie" was added to the reference book and listed as the word of the year. It was unanimously selected because its usage had increased by more than 17,000 percent. What other words have been added to the dictionary? Find out and analyze why you think those words were chosen. Evaluate how they reflect recent changes in culture.

Civics: Photography Ethics

It happens to almost everyone. A friend or someone you know snaps a quick picture at a party, concert, fair, or school event and posts it online. You happened to be in it, and you hate the picture. Maybe you are making a silly face at the time. Perhaps your outfit does not look nearly as great as you thought it did. For whatever reason, you think you look pretty awful. Can you stop the person from posting it all over social media?

Not likely. The general rule on photo taking and sharing (although it can vary from one state to another) is that if you are in a public place, people have the right to take a photo of you and post it online. There are two exceptions to the rule. If you are in a place that implies you will have privacy (like bathrooms, locker rooms, or hospital rooms) and you did not give consent to be photographed

Many people believe that parents shouldn't share photos of their kids on social media.

there, that is a violation of your rights. If the person who took the photo sells it or uses it to make money, that is also not legal.

You Make It, You Own It

Image sharing is done so often and is so easy that it is very difficult to govern. Much of it comes down to common sense and a strong sense of **ethics**. The general rule is that if you took the photo, then you own it. If you took a picture and it is of you (or your room, your food, or anything other than other people), it is your picture.

Since launching, there have been over 40 billion photos and videos shared on Instagram's social network.

On the other hand, thanks to the Digital Millennium **Copyright** Act of 1998, you cannot go online and use a photo from someone else's blog, Instagram, or Facebook post without permission. This violates copyright laws. Giving credit (known as **attribution**) is not enough either. "Picture credit: Joe Smith" is great, but it still breaks the law. You have to have permission to use someone's photo. Often, that is as simple as asking or emailing the person. Many artists are happy to share their work with full credit. But they still have the right to say yes or no.

How can you tell if a photo is copyrighted? Since 1989, people are no longer required to mark it as being copyrighted. So, you have to assume that, if the photo is not from a **public domain** site, it belongs to someone. Don't use it without permission.

Copyright-Free

Millions of free images are available on the internet. The majority of these can be used any way you want, without attribution. Just be sure to check the copyright!

- *Library of Congress*
- *Morguefile*
- *Pexels*
- *Pixabay*
- *Public Domain Archive*
- *Unsplash*

The minimum age to have an account on Instagram is 13 years old, but some kids as young as 8 years old are on it!

Not Really Gone

What if you just delete your photo from a platform? It's gone then, right? According to a study from the IEEE Computer Society, the answer is no. A photo deleted from the internet isn't truly gone. The "deletion-delay phenomenon" means that even if you have deleted a picture, it can still be accessed. If someone has right-clicked on the photo to get and save the **URL**, that person will have access to the picture for days, weeks, or sometimes up to a month. Facebook, Flickr, and Instagram all run this risk. Only Twitter has safeguards built in to prevent it.

An old saying is that a picture is worth a thousand words. Just make sure the words your photos are saying are fair, ethical, and your own.

Developing Claims and Using Evidence

Jennifer Grygiel, a university professor, believes that brands and social media accounts need to disclose whether they're from a real person and should not participate in "mass deception." What does that mean? Go online and read about Lil Miquela, a 19-year-old on Instagram who models high-end clothes, supports social causes, and shares her favorite hair products. Since 2016, she has gotten over 1 million followers. In April 2018, the world found out Lil Miquela is not actually a real person. She is a "digital supermodel," a computer-generated image created by a company specializing in robotics. Should companies make it clear if someone is real or a robot? What do you think? Make a claim and be sure to gather evidence to support your thoughts.

Economics: Internet Advertising

Did you know that businesses, not young people, are the ones that are using social image-sharing platforms more often every year? In summer 2017, there were 15 million profiles of businesses on Instagram. By mid-2018, that number had already reached 25 million. As many companies advertise on these sites, even more Instagrammers follow those businesses. They learn about new products and services.

Why are businesses flocking to these sites? The answer is simple: money. Companies that specialize in visual products, such as fashion and food, do especially well on sites like Instagram.

Studies indicate that in 2018, about 70 percent of U.S. companies will use Instagram for marketing purposes.

In 2017, these companies spent $4 billion on Instagram, and, according to experts, by 2019 that number will more than double to $10 billion.

The Influencers

By putting ads on image-sharing sites like Snapchat and Instagram, companies can build **brand awareness** and introduce new products in a unique way. It gives businesses the chance to communicate directly with consumers all over the world. Businesses can quickly build a large audience and often see sales

Communicating Conclusions

Before you read this book, did you think about the pictures you posed for or posted online? Has what you have learned changed what you post? Share what you have learned with others. Look at the pictures you have on your profiles and ask yourself if the other people in those photos agreed to be in them. How might they feel about being it? Analyze what role sharing photos plays in your life and how important it is (or is not) to you.

About 60 percent of Instagram users confirmed they've learned about a service or product from using the social platform.

About 87 percent of Pinterest users purchased something they've pinned.

explode when they partner with celebrities, sports stars, or everyday people with a large following. These people are known as influencers.

Influencers are people on social media who have the power to impact consumers' purchase decisions. Some have this effect because they are experts on a specific topic, while others are simply famous for taking great photos! They typically have thousands to millions of followers.

Taking Informed Action

Recent research states that social media is extremely addictive and negatively impacts young people's mental health. The study found that image-sharing sites were the most damaging for creating feelings of inadequacy and anxiety, often since many photos are filtered and edited to make people look "perfect." In April 2018, Instagram created a Wellbeing Team. Leader Eva Chen stated, "Making the community a safer place, a place where people feel good, is a huge priority for Instagram." Experts believe that sites should mark photos that have been significantly **airbrushed**. They also recommend sites have pop-up warnings when users have reached a level of social media usage considered potentially harmful. Talk to your friends about these ideas. Do you agree or disagree? What changes would you like to see?

Pinterest ads don't look like ads—they look like real pins!

In 2018, some of the most successful influencers (and their **net worth**) include:

Influencer	Number of Followers
Huda Kattan • *Makeup and beauty expert* • *Net worth: $4.5 million*	*Twitter: 131,000* *Instagram: 25.8 million* *Facebook: 4.8 million*
Lele Pons • *Actress, singer, and* **vlogger** • *Net worth: $3 million*	*Twitter: 1.89 million* *Instagram: 25.3 million* *Facebook: 3.9 million*
Zach King • *Vlogger* • *Net worth: $3 million*	*Twitter: 179,000* *Instagram: 21.6 million* *Facebook: 3.8 million*
Cameron Dallas • *Actor and vlogger* • *Net worth: $4.5 million*	*Twitter: 16.5 million* *Instagram: 21 million* *Facebook: 3.7 million*

Sharing images has evolved from showing off your family vacation photos to something so much bigger!

Think About It

Instagram, one of the internet's biggest image-sharing websites, has more than 800 million active users. More than 95 million photos are uploaded to the site every day! The majority of users are between 18 and 29 years old, and females use the site more often than males. Almost a third of teens state Instagram is the most important social network, and half of the site's users access the platform at least once a day. What do these facts tell you about the role of image-sharing in today's culture?

For More Information

FURTHER READING

Bernhardt, Carolyn. *Snap It! Snapchat Projects for the Real World.* Minneapolis: Checkerboard Library, 2017.

Furgang, Adam. *Snap and Share: Exploring the Potential of Instagram and Other Photo and Video Apps.* New York: Rosen Publishing, 2015.

Mattern, Joanne. *Instagram.* Minneapolis: Checkerboard Library, 2017.

Panaccione, Nancy. *Instagram It!* Longwood, FL: Fine Print Publishing, 2016.

Rajczak Nelson, Kristen. *Instagram: Kevin Systrom and Mike Krieger.* New York: Rosen Publishing, 2015.

Spalding, Madeleine. *Snapchat.* Minneapolis: Checkerboard Library, 2017.

WEBSITES

The New York Times—Rules for Social Media, Created by Kids
www.nytimes.com/2017/01/05/well/family/the-unspoken-rules-kids-create-for-instagram.html
Read about the rules for using social media that were created for and written by kids.

KidsHealth—Online Safety
https://kidshealth.org/en/kids/online-id.html
Learn about how to stay safe online.

GLOSSARY

airbrushed (AIR-bruhshd) edited to remove flaws and enhance an image

attribution (ah-truh-BYOO-shuhn) credit given for something

brand awareness (BRAND uh-WAIR-nis) how familiar consumers are with a brand of goods or services

copyright (KAH-pee-rite) the legal right to be the only one to reproduce, publish, or sell the contents and form of a literary, musical, or artistic work

developed (dih-VEL-uhpd) exposed film to chemicals in order to produce a visible image

ethics (ETH-iks) rules of behavior based on ideas about what is good and bad

filters (FIL-terz) apps and features that allow photos to be altered or added to

GIFs (GIFS) image file formats; stands for "graphic interchange format"

millennials (muh-LEN-ee-uhlz) people born in the 1980s or 1990s

net worth (NET WURTH) how much a person owns (assets) minus what the person owes to others (liabilities or debt)

public domain (PUHB-lik doh-MAYN) free for use by the public

running of the bulls (RUHN-ing OV THUH BUHLZ) an event where people run through the streets of the city of Pamplona trying to stay ahead of bulls

selfie (SELF-ee) a photo taken of oneself

URL (YOO-AHR-EL) an internet address

vlogger (VLAWG-er) a person who posts video blogs

INDEX

advertising, 22–29

cameras, 4–5, 6, 7
celebrities, 12, 27, 29
cell phones, 6, 7, 9
copyright, 18–19

economics, 22–29
ethics, 16–21

Facebook, 7, 18, 21, 29
film, 4–5
Flickr, 21

geography, 10–15

image-sharing platforms
    advertising, 22–24
    celebrities on, 12
    dangers of, 27
    ethics of, 16–21
    history of, 4–9
    selfies, 10–15
    statistics, 6
influencers, 24–29
Instagram, 10, 12, 27
    and advertisements,
        22–24, 25
    deleted photos, 21
    influencers, 29
    minimum age to have
        account, 20
    statistics, 18, 30
internet, 6, 19, 30
    advertising, 22–29
    deleted photos, 20–21

millennials, 10–11

photos, 4–9. *See also*
    image-sharing platforms
Pinterest, 9, 26, 28
public domain, 19

selfie sticks, 15
selfies, 4, 10–15
    first ones, 13
    and millennials, 10–11
    where the most are taken,
        12, 14
Shutterfly, 7
Snapchat, 24
social media, 6, 9, 14, 16,
    17, 21, 27

Twitter, 12, 21, 29